LIVING WORDS

Other works by Michel Quoist
Prayers of Life
The Christian Response
Christ is Alive
Meet Christ and Live

Contents

Contents

Foreword

The words that make up this volume were first spoken on television and a great number of viewers asked me to publish them in book form. At first I was reluctant but not, as might be imagined, through any feelings of humility. Like most people who express themselves in one way or another, I am happy when people who tell me that they have been helped by my sermons ask me for the text. But therein lies the problem — these are, precisely, sermons and televised at that. They were written to be heard and not read, and I am always afraid that very few people will find in a reading of these sermons what was experienced and understood when listening to them. Furthermore, in the context of the mass of 'The Lord's Day' on television, I was addressing several million viewers from all walks of life and of different cultures, many of whom did not completely share my faith. I made an effort to express myself as simply as possible with the help of concrete images and examples but without detracting from the depth and meaning of my message, so as to reach as many people as possible.

Loftier minds will perhaps confuse simplicity with simpleness. But then, if more modest ones are able to understand me, it doesn't really matter.

These texts, however, should not be taken as 'examples' of homilies. While taking the Gospel as my base, and I hope without straying from it, I have attempted in some of them to answer questions which had been put to me (for instance, on the younger generation, the feast of the Holy Family or changes within the Church, the feast of the Holy Trinity). But there again, there was no question of treating the whole subject — how could I have done that in ten minutes of television time? — but simply of offering a few basic reflections to clarify the subject.

Finally, I sometimes refer to certain topical events which I have not modified here. They are part of my constant efforts to try to root the message of the Gospel in present-day living.

Thus, in spite of all these reservations, I hand these texts over to you. May they at least help a few of you to reach and know Jesus Christ a little better, the living Word of the Father, who I hope can give reason and meaning to all our lives.

What are you Living for?[1]

The Gospel of Jesus Christ according to
St Matthew — 4:1 — 11

Then Jesus was led by the Spirit out into the wilderness to be tempted by the devil. He fasted for forty days and forty nights, after which he was very hungry, and the tempter came and said to him, 'If you are the Son of God, tell these stones to turn into loaves.' But he replied, 'Scripture says: Man does not live by bread alone but on every word that comes from the mouth of God.' The devil then took him to the holy city and made him stand on the parapet of the Temple. 'If you are the Son of God' he said 'throw yourself down; for scripture says: "He will put you in his angels' charge, and they will support you on their hands in case you hurt your foot against a stone."' Jesus said to him, 'Scripture also says: "You must not put the Lord your God to the test."' Next, taking him to a very high mountain, the devil showed him all the kingdoms of the world and their splendour. 'I will give you all these' he said, 'if you fall at my feet and worship me.' Then Jesus replied, 'Be off Satan! For scripture says: "You must worship the Lord your God and serve him alone".' Then the devil left him, and angels appeared and looked after him.

1. Homily for the First Sunday of Lent.

A man goes to a railway station and asks the booking clerk for 'A railway ticket please!'

'Where to?' inquires the clerk.

'I don't know, I just want a ticket!' the man replies.

What would you think of such a request? You would surely think that the man was a bit deranged!

Sometimes we are like that man. I mean, we don't always know where we are going, or the purpose of our lives.

What are you living for? Many would answer that they were living for their children; others would add that they wanted to build a better world. But what world? And what do you want for your children?

For Christians, Lent is a privileged time when we can reconfirm our life's goal and make new choices. Choices which are often painful and demand sacrifices from us.

Jesus too had to make sacrifices. He was a man as other men. He didn't play at being a man; he didn't 'pretend' to be a man. It was gradually, through prayer and meditation, in the presence of his Father, that he began to understand the mission he was meant to carry out. Throughout his life he was dreadfully tempted to impose himself as other men do, through power and might. But God does not impose, he proposes, because he loves man and he does not force him. Jesus often needed to repeat to himself, in the silence, in the 'desert,' that he was not on earth for his personal benefit, but that he had been sent by his Father for the good of his brothers, to liberate them from their individual and collective alienation and to enable them to acknowledge together, beyond temporal happiness (but without excluding it), an unimaginable dignity, that of the Son of God.

Several of his disciples collected and condensed their own unique and symbolic accounts of Jesus' struggle to remain faithful to his mission — we have just seen an extract from St Matthew — and if we reflect on the three temptations he was faced with, we shall find that they are also ours.

The temptation of consumption

The first temptation is one I shall call 'the temptation of consumption'; 'If you want, you can change these stones into bread,' — that is, if you want, you can feed all men. They suffer and they hunger, they have no work; you can alleviate their material misery. You can perform miracles, the 'economic miracle'!

'Man shall not live on bread alone,' Jesus replies, 'but by every word that proceeds out of the mouth of God.'

Let us understand this well: Jesus is asking us to dissociate ourselves from earthly gains. In his prayer, he teaches us to say: 'Our Father who art in heaven . . . give us this day our daily bread.' We must fight for this daily bread, to say nothing of a pat of butter. We must fight for ourselves, for our brothers, for all mankind. But what he asks of us is that we fight against this alienating consumerism and against the illusory belief that this is where happiness lies. Jesus tells us that our heart needs a different kind of nourishment. Parents, who daily discover the needs of your children, who know how much they need not only material well-being but your time, you attention, your words, your love, you surely understand what I mean.

Like the child, man needs God's love, his Father who has spoken and who has something to say to everyone. As long as men do not hear his word and as long as they do not live by it, they will open their mouths (whether physical or spiritual) wider and consume even more. They can even form a society consecrated to consumer products, but deep down there will always be a gnawing hunger that will turn them into malnourished, anguished people simply because they are starving and they don't know what they are starving for — or rather who they are starving for.

They are poor children who do not know their father; poor children born of an unknown father!

I am sure that you agree, that you are saying: 'It's true, the world is mad! So is society.' But we forget that we are part of this society and that we are participants in this madness. We are *all* slaves of consumerism.

Think of that little god, your car. Think of the comforts of home, your children's toys stacked in a cupboard while they prefer to play with an old shoe box; the books and magazines which will never be read; the masses of records which are getting more expensive all the time and which do not satisfy any more; his innumerable expensive ties, her many silk scarves . . . and so on and so forth.

We hunger for bread. Do we hunger for God?

The temptation of power

The second temptation of Jesus is the temptation of Power, to put his Father's power to personal use. He resists: 'You shall not tempt the Lord your God.' That is, you shall not ask God for favours; you are the one who must serve. The strength of Jesus lies in the fact that he put himself entirely at the disposal and service of his Father and brothers.

We are tempted to use God, to have him on our side (I was going to say 'in our pocket') individually and collectively.

Collectively, through the ages, many human groupings — nations, races, states, governments, armies and political parties — have tried, and are still trying, to use Christians, the Church, and God to their own ends with slogans such as 'God be with Us,' 'Christians be with Us,' for Victory, Order, Revolution.

Individually, we often recite the *Our Father* in re-
verse: 'Our Father who art in heaven, *my* will be
done.' We become the centre of things, we usurp
God's place. Inevitably, many people then turn away
from God because he has not obeyed them.

The temptation of idolatry

The third temptation is that of idolatry. At this
point, you are perhaps saying to yourself: 'This time,
it doesn't concern me because it's to do with pagans
who worshipped idols in ancient times.'

Alas, the world is full of idols — from that huge
idol called Money which we all more or less worship
even if we are trying to topple it off the pedestal to
which the 'system' has elevated it — to the myriad
little idols in front of which we prostrate ourselves
daily: our package of cigarettes or our cream buns;
such and such a singer; television; fashion; our
bodies or someone else's body. And at a deeper level,
we worship our ideas, our ideologies . . . All these little pieces of ourselves which kneel before these stand-
in gods cause us gradually, and sometimes uncon-
sciously, to live prostrate, flat on our faces, incapable of getting up and living upright and prostrating
ourselves (this time of our own volition) before God.

The Holy Spirit can guide us to the desert too. In
the midst of the noise of our actions or in the silence
of our hearts, he beckons us.

Even today, because we have come to church, or because we have switched on our television sets, Jesus Christ speaks to us through his Gospel. He asks: "What happiness are you fighting for? What kind of a world are you building? Are you exploiting God, or are you, rather, serving him and your brothers?"

Today, my friends, Jesus Christ is asking us 'What are you living for? What is the purpose of your lives?'

Who do you think Jesus Christ is?[1]

The Gospel of Jesus Christ according to
St Matthew — 16:13 — 19

When Jesus came to the region of Caesarea Philippi he put this question to his disciples, 'Who do people say the Son of Man is?' And they said, 'Some say he is John the Baptist, some Elijah, and others Jeremiah or one of the prophets.' 'But you,' he said, 'who do you say I am?' Then Simon Peter spoke up, 'You are the Christ,' he said 'the Son of the Living God.' Jesus replied, 'Simon son of Jonah, you are a happy man! Because it was not flesh and blood that revealed this to you but my Father in Heaven. So I now say to you: You are Peter and on this rock I will build my Church. And the gates of the underworld can never hold out against it. I will give you the keys of the kingdom of heaven: whatever you loose on earth shall be considered loosed in heaven.

As you can see, opinion polls were not invented by politicians. Two thousand years ago, Jesus himself used them. Of course he did not hire the services of

1. Homily for the feast of St Peter and St Paul.

Gallup or Harris — he canvassed his disciples directly: 'Who do people say I am?' he asked them. 'Who
do they think I am?' And they answered, 'Some say
you are John the Baptist; some, Elijah; and others
Jeremiah or one of the prophets.' 'And you,' Jesus
asked, 'Who do you say I am?' 'Christ, the Son of
the Living God,' Peter replied.

People in power always worry about their image,
their popularity. Did Christ have any such worries?
Not in the least. On the contrary, the Gospel shows
us a Christ who always refused the admiration of
people who wanted to make him king. He was preoccupied with the success of his mission — did mankind understand what he had come to accomplish?
Had they discovered his true identity? He had joined
humanity unobtrusively, incognito, so as not to impose himself through power and might but to reach
the weak and the poor.

'Who do you say I am?' Jesus' question still
stands, and has stood at the core of history and of
man's heart for twenty centuries. And it crops up in
thousands of books, conferences, discussions — on
radio and television. It is the essential question, fixed
in time like an immense invitation to love — no one
can escape it.

'Who do you say I am?' The question must be
answered. I won't go into the historian's reply, which
is too brief and incomplete. I shall also gloss over the
answer that Jesus was a great man, a prophet. But I

shall dwell on the Christian's answer which operates
on two levels: first, that Jesus is the son of God but
belongs to the past; and second, that Jesus is the son
of God and belongs to the present.

The mind and the heart

I respect the historian's view because it is a necessary one. But on its own, it can provide only endless
questions which lead nowhere. It is impossible to
study Jesus in a history book; it is only possible to
study him by making him a part of our daily experience, in our personal and communal lives within the
Church. Intellectual knowledge is not real knowledge. Would you claim to 'know' your spouse if all
the information you had were a passport and some
childhood memories as retold by his or her friends?
You know your spouse because you live together, because you share your work, your joy and your sadness . . . and most of all because you love each other.
'Only the eyes of the heart really know' says St
Exupéry's Little Prince.

Faith is reasonable — but it is not a form of
'proof.' *God invites us* — Jesus said to Peter who
had recognized him, 'For flesh and blood have not
revealed it to you but my Father in heaven' — God
invites us to this faith which is a meeting of love,
while at the same time allowing us space for freedom
and risk.

Jesus Christ is more than just a prophet

Today, as 2,000 years ago, many believe that Jesus was a prophet. An extraordinary man who preached and practiced the most beautiful message of love that this world has ever known. I often meet people who believe that Christ was a prophet and I say to them:

'Draw life from this message and you will build yourselves; stalwart and united with others of good faith, you will build a world of justice and peace. And if you are honest and receptive, you will perhaps discover a mysterious force at the core of your lives and your actions for your fellow human beings. And at the center of this force, an infinite love will beckon you. Then you will perhaps see the shape of a face emerge and you will know that it is he — the Lord, Son of the Living God.'

Jesus Christ — man of the past or man of the present?

Finally there are the Christians. No more intelligent or better than others but who, in the wake of Peter and countless disciples throughout history, recognize and have absolute faith in Jesus. This is what Christian faith is all about. It is not merely a belief in God (millions of people believe in God without being Christians), but a firm belief in Jesus of Nazareth. It is the decision freely taken that this man was neither a clown nor a liar or madman. It is discovering in him someone more than a prophet, someone who came to reveal God to us by showing himself: 'He who sees me sees the Father,' someone who came to liberate us individually and collectively, who died and was resurrected so that we could be renewed in a new world. This is where the two levels of faith, which I mentioned earlier, come in: belief in Jesus as a man of the past, or belief of Jesus as a man of the present.

When in an assembly of Christians I ask: 'According to you, where was Jesus Christ resurrected to?' inevitably there is a long embarrassed silence. Then someone finally speaks up: 'To the sky,' signalling upwards with a movement of the head.

To the sky? What does that mean? Up there in the clouds? Well, no. Jesus resurrected lives among us, not in a physical sense of course as 2,000 years ago in Palestine but nevertheless in an absolutely real sense. He foretold it:

'Know that I am with you always; yes to the end of time.'

'Where two or three meet in my name I shall be there with them.'

'If anyone loves me he will keep my word, and my Father will love him and we shall come to him and make our home with him.'

'I tell you solemnly, in so far as you did this to one of the least of these brothers of mine, you did it to me.'

This is the major demarcation line between Christians who believe in a past-tense Christ resurrected 'up to the sky' in the sense of having left this earth, and those who believe in Christ, present tense, resurrected but living today among us.

The first group tends to rely completely on a concept of religion that unites man to God who is 'in heaven' and 'in the past.' They faithfully follow all religious ceremonies, which to them are commemorations of past events: the birth of Christ at Christmas, the main points in his life, and his death on Good Friday. They will pray, their eyes lifted to heaven, to ask him *above* for forgiveness for those *down below* who walk in 'this vale of tears' while awaiting entry into their 'real home,' the Kingdom of Heaven. The more virtuous ones try to imitate the life of Christ, their Brother and Model, who is no longer among them.

The second group also adore their 'Father who is in Heaven' but it is in this world, and with the same faith, that they search for Jesus, dead and resurrected, living today among them, inviting them to join him, 'incarnating' themselves too and uniting with him (and not just by imitating him), to work with him in the reign of the Father who is 'already among us' as Christ said. They do not celebrate the 'memory' of Christ but his mystery unfolding itself daily in the history of man, the mystery of which they are a part, with and in his Church.

Jesus among men? That's hardly fitting!

The idea of a God living among mankind complicates everything! One can well understand why many people would be tempted (excuse the pun) to send him back to where he came from, in the same way as you would deal with that inevitable person in your neighborhood who is forever knocking at your door asking for a favor, or your signature on a petition, or your membership in an association, to whom you politely show the door . . . and close it on him to preserve your peace.

To admit that God came as a man among us is itself very difficult. But in the eyes of many good people, it's certainly not fitting that he apparently did not wish to 'cling to his equality with God,' as St Paul tells us, 'but emptied himself to assume the condition of a slave.' It is for this reason that a lot of good souls 'defend' God and fight . . . to have him reinstated. They can turn a blind eye to that 'folly' of 33 years, but that in his excessive love for mankind, he should be obstinate to the point of 'living among them,' of *identifying* with prisoners, the starving, the homeless, and all poor people . . . to the extent that one can't go out of doors without bumping into him, is just too much. One can't go to work, to school, shopping, a union meeting or even a political rally! . . . without having him under one's nose and hearing his perpetual murmur, 'Whatever you do to the least of my followers, it is to me that you do it!' All this becomes unbearable because it changes everything in the Christian heart. And yet, this is what true faith is!

My friends, Jesus Christ is asking us, 'Who do you think I am?'

Would that we could humbly reply: 'O Jesus, I admit secretly that I would have preferred you to have been a prophet, I would have preferred you to have abandoned Earth for Heaven. It would be so much easier.

'But I believe with all my strength that you are the Son of the living God.

'I believe with all my strength that you are among us spreading your infinite mystery.

'Thus I who want to be your disciple come towards you to meet you and to try to work with you and all my brothers of good will so as to save man and to save the world!'

Christmas, or Love has Taken Root on Earth[1]

Beginning of the Gospel of Jesus Christ according to St John — 1:1 — 18

In the beginning was the Word: and the Word was with God and the Word was God. He was with God in the beginning. Through him all things came to be, not one thing had its being but through him. All that came to be had life in him and that life was the light of men, a light that shines in the dark, a light that darkness could not overpower.

A man came, sent by God. His name was John. He came as a witness, as witness to speak for the light, so that everyone might believe through him. He was not the light, only a witness to speak for the light.

The Word was the true light that enlightens all men; and he was coming into the world. He was in the world that had its being through him, and the world did not know him. He came to his own domain and his own people did not accept him. But to all who did accept him he gave power to become children of God, to all who believe in the name of him who was born not out of human stock or urge of the flesh or

1. Homily for Christmas Day.

will of man but of God himself. The Word was made flesh, he lived among us, and we saw his glory, the glory that is his as the only Son of the Father, full of grace and truth.

John appears as his witness. He proclaims: 'This is the one of whom I said: He who comes after me ranks before me because he existed before me.'

Indeed from his fullness we have, all of us, received — yes graces in return for grace, since, though the Law was given through Moses, grace and truth have come through Jesus Christ. No one has ever seen God; it is the only Son, who is nearest to the Father's heart, who has made him known.

Two thousand years ago on this night, Caesar Augustus Emperor of Rome ruled 'the whole earth' — so goes the Gospel. Have you heard of Caesar Augustus?

Today, as every year, the whole world has stopped, not because of Emperor Augustus but because of a baby born 2,000 years ago whose name was Jesus.

It's Christmas!

Christmas today has changed — it's become commercialized and pagan. Everyone agrees on that. It's become a time of excessive eating and spending; a time to trap sentimental people into overspending on gifts, trimming pine trees and breaking open the bubbly. But I won't dwell on this, not because I ignore these deviations and perversions but because I know that when thick smoke rises and catches in your throat and brings tears to your eyes it's because a fire has been lit.

Come with me to see the fire

This fire is an irresistible leap of love which today is felt in every heart and is expressed (however clumsily sometimes) through gift offerings — a doll, a train set, a glittering array of clothes, chocolates and mince pies.

It is that feeling of forgiving affection which inspires us to invite Aunt Matilda over even though we are no longer on speaking terms because of her gossiping. And it makes us invite old Grandpa too even though he's going to bore everyone by repeating his story about Christmas in the trenches for the hundredth time.

It is that burst of affection which even crosses prison walls where things are a bit better on this special day and the arms on that particular battlefield are laid down for a few hours.

But it's short-lived, some of you will say. True, but name one other birthday that can inspire so much love on earth every year. Others will insist that people don't know what they're celebrating. That's true too but does the fire in the hearth burn less because we don't know the hand that lit it?

My friends, since the coming of Jesus a fire has been burning on earth.

What exactly is this fire whose Christmas flame is a sign of his mysterious presence in the heart of man?

He is the burning fire on earth

As with everyone else, my teens were a time of searching for some sort of meaning to my life. What was the purpose of living?

I remember stopping in front of a bookshop window, fascinated by the cover of a book on display. The title was spread over it in large letters, I WANT TO SEE GOD. And I said to myself, 'If he exists, I want to see him too, to know him, to talk to him. But where do I find him?' Later I was to find out that the child whose birth we are celebrating today, told his friends, 'No one has ever seen God!' But he also added that 'Whoever sees me sees the Father,' and 'No one reaches the Father except through me.' Then I understood that you could meet God only in Jesus Christ. But was I to continue my search? Who was God? Was he simply the Source, what the philosophers call the First Cause?

I learned from St John that God 'is' love. *Love itself.* And that is why when he came on earth, he did not appear as an almighty master, but in a stable, a little naked baby, his only riches being an infinite love. This realization came to me like a shock: God was love and Jesus was love incarnate.

My friends, it is he, the fire burning on earth. That's what Christmas is.

Love does not constrain, it liberates

But why must this happy occasion be tinged with sadness? Alas, it is also a time when we are more aware of the suffering in the world. It's because the stronger the warmth is, the crueller the cold seems. Two-thirds of the world's population suffer from hunger; millions of people have no jobs, no homes, no freedom. The amount of arms and weapons capable of destroying the world grows and grows.

What is this love that causes so much suffering?

'It's not love, it's the lack of it.'

'Then let God give it to us!'

But love can't be imposed, it can only offer itself. Where would love be if it said 'I want you to love me, I'll force you to love me!' Man's terrible greatness lies in that he is free to refuse God's love, to refuse to love his brothers as God has asked him. And God can't force us because love is not constraining, it's liberating.

I don't want to be a puppet on a string manipulated by a God who would program my life, leaving no room for risk.

I don't want a God who would build a just world in place of man.

I don't want a God who would prevent me from doing evil while allowing me to do good.

I want to be free to choose whether I want to punch someone on the nose or shake his hand, because without that freedom I would never know if, when I offer my hand, I'm offering my friendship.

I want to be free, not through arrogance but because I want to love and be loved.

Love is a battle

And so, the fire of life is burning on earth but the earth isn't catching fire. Has love clashed with man's liberty and thus failed? Was Jesus wrong in not being a dictator, in coming to us with empty hands and leaving in the same manner to return to his Father?

I'll end with two observations.

The first is that Jesus has only just come among us. His arrival, in the context of the history of the world, took place only yesterday. We forget that we are only at the beginning of Christianity and that no fruit can mature unless the seed germinates first.

The second observation is that if Christ has planted the seed then, with him, we must nurture the plant. The victory of love is total in the life of Jesus but ours is the responsibility for forging this love in time.

We must, in the same way as the Virgin Mary a long long time ago, say *yes* to the daily annunciations. All our lives, every new morning, this *yes* waits to be touched by love to make it bloom. Otherwise no man, no institution, no structure or society can hope to be built upright and solid.

Don't think for one moment that this is just an idealist's golden dream and that it's easy to love. Love is a battle, its criterion of authenticity is 'other people.' As Jesus said, 'Love your brother as you would love yourself.' This means simply that we must want for others what we want for ourselves, for example:

—We want to have enough to eat, then we must also want everyone to have enough to eat and work to that end.

—We want work, an honest salary, a home, schools for our children, a dignified and respected old age, then we must want these same good things for all our brothers.

So tell me my friends, do you think it's as easy to fight for others as it is to fight for ourselves alone? And when we're fighting, is it easy to do it for love? No. It's as false to have a so-called love which doesn't need any effort as it is to engage in a battle without experiencing love. In fact, because of the weight of the selfishness and pride which we come up against in ourselves and the world around us, that is, sin, loving means being exposed and vulnerable in our fight for others and being crucified by them.

The child of Christmas didn't escape this tragic battle, but in him and by him, love emerged triumphant!

Yes my friends, since the coming of Jesus, a fire has been burning on earth. A fire that will never die. The naked babe of Christmas opened up another story within the world's story, an epic of love triumphing over selfishness, injustice, pride and hate. An epic of unending, eternal love.

So light your candles, offer your gifts, eat your Christmas pudding and sing! Love has taken root in the world and we believe it with all our strength. It will flower because millions of us believe it, because this love is a person and that person is God . . . Emmanuel, God is with us: Happy Christmas!

No Prophet is ever Accepted in his own Country[1]

The Gospel of Jesus Christ according to
St Luke — 4:21 — 30

[At the Temple of Nazareth after the reading from
the Book of Isaiah, Jesus declared . . .]

'This text is being fulfilled today even as you listen.'
And he won the approval of all, and they were aston-
ished by the gracious words that came from his lips.

They said, 'This is Joseph's son, surely?' But he re-
plied, 'No doubt you will quote me the saying, "Phy-
sician, heal yourself" and tell me, "We have heard
all that happened in Capernaum, do the same here in
your own countryside".' And he went on, 'I tell you
solemnly, no prophet is ever accepted in his own
country.

'There were many widows in Israel, I can assure
you, in Elijah's day, when heaven remained shut for
three years and six months and a great famine raged
throughout the land, but Elijah was not sent to any
of these: he was sent to a widow at Zarephath, a
Sidonian town. And in the prophet Elisha's time

1. Homily for the Fourth Sunday in Ordinary Time.

*there were many lepers in Israel, but none of these
was cured, except the Syrian, Naaman.*

*When they heard this everyone in the synagogue
was enraged. They sprang to their feet and hustled
him out of the town; and they took him up to the
brow of the hill their town was built on, intending to
throw him down the cliff, but he slipped through the
crowd and walked away.*

Nothing goes right any more . . . The honeymoon is
over and they already want to kill him! Yet it had all
started so well.

Back in his native country, Jesus returned to the
temple of his childhood which he used to attend regu-
larly. But on that day, in his sermon, he made a vio-
lent attack. This is the substance of what he said to
the faithful:

1. In fact, your interest is to 'profit' from me.

2. Strangers and pagans are more disinterested
and thus more open than you. It is to them that I
must go.

Well, put yourself in their place. Admittedly it is
an infuriating sermon. We would have reacted the
same way. Of course, we wouldn't have dragged our
parish priest to the top of a tower with the purpose of
throwing him down . . . but we certainly react in the
same way in a verbal manner: 'These priests today!
They've a nerve to criticize us and call us bad Christians, we the faithful of the parish. And the 'good'
Christians are naturally those outside the parish who
are nothing like us!'

Self-interested Christians

First of all, let us examine our conscience. Are we not Christians out of self-interest and habit? We are like the congregation at the temple, we accept the Lord but on the condition that he uses his power for our benefit. In fact, what we want is a God who is an indulgence-bank on which we can draw the checks we need; we want a God who fulfills the desires we ourselves cannot satisfy; we want a God who can give us a better world without our having to dirty our hands working for it — otherwise 'What good is religion?'

We are making a tragic mistake. God isn't a supermarket for indulgences, or some kind of sugar-daddy or an all-risk insurance policy. He isn't a 'providential' political leader for the foundation of a just society or a genial Minister of Finance for economic miracles. He is first and foremost a loving Father who waits to be loved freely by his sons.

Let us not make any mistakes here, otherwise the Lord will repeat his words to the faithful at the temple that no prophet is well received in his own country, and he'll turn his back on us, leaving us to the indifference of our good conscience and our miles of selfish prayers.

The 'Habitués of God'

My friends, are we not also very often 'habitués' of God? Now, habit is a scourge which paralyses and ends up snuffing out all life.

You all know some habitues of love, for instance. Perhaps even you yourselves have been frightened to find that one day you have nothing to say to each other, you are bored. And then you think, well, at least we have the children to occupy us, to distract us . . .

It's so terribly sad — habitués of love where love has slowly waned and faded away to nothing.

The same happens with religion — habitué Christians! For many people, God is like an old relative inherited by generation after generation, one that doesn't really cause any problems until the day when we perhaps look a little closer. 'It was at our wedding/when grandmother died/the baptism of our first born . . . that we noticed. It was a great shock!' we declare.

Or else when we were younger, we were perhaps part of a religious youth movement. And so on.

Little by little, God has become 'Someone.' He came to us in the form of Jesus Christ and we understood that this Christ was not to be found in the graveyard of history but in life itself where he daily awaits us. So we formed a relationship with him and perhaps we even worked together in the Christian community and the human community generally. And then, it became a case of 'Well you know how it is, the pressures of work, the daily worries . . . we lost touch.' And like two friends who haven't seen each other for a long time, when they eventually see each other in a crowd, they barely recognize each other.

'Habitué' Christians who don't know, or have forgotten their God, are a sad thing.

To practice or not to practice

I see two attitudes here. There are people who insist on certain religious habits, certain practices and prayers which they want to pass on to their children because they feel their children should be raised the way they themselves were raised. Others, particularly among younger people, find it both ridiculous and hypocritical to go through rituals which, for them, have lost all meaning. And they maintain that one can believe without having to practice a religion.

Both attitudes are wrong. Just as the motions of love *without* the sentiment are a degrading and odious caricature, it is true to say that any practice of religion in a general sense *without* a true encounter with the living Christ is a terrible comedy if not a tragic illusion. What would you think of a couple in love who said 'We are madly in love but we don't talk to each other anymore, we don't kiss and we have separate rooms?'

So what do we do when we have become 'habitués' of God? Drop it and forget all about it? No. Continue the way you are, whatever your ups and downs, your doubts and your trials, because true love is measured by its durability. *But* through all your actions and movements, do all you can to find the living Jesus Christ who is the source as well as the end.

My friends, if our faith, the outward signs of our faith, and our obligations are declining, it is because the face of Jesus Christ is vanishing from our sight.

Salvation for all

After the examination of conscience, I said I would propose a short reflection on salvation. Here it is.

At the temple, Jesus clearly affirmed the universality of his mission — to the Jews this was scandalous. But there was worse. Not only did Christ go among strangers and pagans, he also gave priority to sinners and poor people. Look at it this way: Jesus took his meals with thieves and smugglers; he conversed with corrupt officials and forgave them; he talked with prostitutes and told these little ladies of the night that they would 'precede us in the Kingdom.' It is to the beggar, the vagrant who might even be a murderer, that he opens the gates of Paradise first.

There's the scandal! It seems that Jesus ignores the religious and moral habits of those he reveals himself to. Why? Because the most important thing is their faith in his person, 'Whoever believes in me will have eternal life.'

But what is even more disturbing because it seems so contradictory, is Jesus at the famous scene of the Last Judgment. You will recall his words: I was hungry, I was thirsty, I was a stranger, sick, in prison, etc. and you helped me or didn't help me. (see Matthew 25:35 — 44).

Jesus is pointing out that those who were saved as well as those who were condemned didn't know that the person they had accepted or rejected was *himself*. We will therefore be judged solely on the way we have behaved towards our brothers.

For many of you, this is a kind of consolation because it hurts you to see, among your loved ones, those who either don't know Jesus Christ or have ceased to know him. Consequently you can assure yourself that it they truly live for others Jesus will welcome them. He himself said: 'Come, blessed of my Father . . . because I hungered and you gave me food . . .'

Why must Jesus Christ be made known?

The question poses itself. If, to be saved, it is enough to put ourselves entirely at the service of our brothers, do we need to make Jesus Christ known? Do we benefit more from knowing him?

I myself found the answer following a painful but beautiful episode.[1] I know a woman whose baby had been torn away from her during the war. Later she found out that the baby was alive and had grown up into a young man. After a long search, he was finally located and one day, his mother told me of the scene of the reunion. She was sitting down, overcome with emotion, with her son on his knees before her, caressing her face with trembling fingers. 'You're my mother, you're my mother,' he repeated. Then suddenly I understood. For twenty years this boy had been the son of this mother. He had everything since she had given him life. Yet he had nothing because he didn't know the source of that life. He didn't know

---

1. Already described in *Christ is Alive*, p. 135, Gill and Macmillan, Dublin 1971.

the face of his mother. He didn't know her name. He had no way of returning the love she had given him.

If there were only one man on earth who didn't know Jesus Christ but lived like Christ himself simply because he loved his brothers, everything would have to be done all the same to enable him to encounter and get to know Christ. Because living is beautiful, being saved is beautiful, being loved is beautiful, but it is all tragically incomplete as long as we don't know who to thank for it.

My friends, Jesus Christ gives to all men. But he waits for us to return *everything,* freely, through our actions.

Listen to the 'Other,'
Listen to God[1]

The Gospel of Jesus Christ according to
St Luke — 10:38 — 42

*In the course of their journey he came to a village,
and a woman named Martha welcomed him into her
house. She had a sister called Mary, who sat down at
the Lord's feet and listened to him speaking. Now
Martha who was distracted with all the serving said,
'Lord, do you not care that my sister is leaving me to
do the serving all by myself? Please tell her to help
me.' But the Lord answered: 'Martha, Martha,' he
said 'you worry and fret about so many things, and
yet few are needed, indeed only one. It is Mary who
has chosen the better part; it is not to be taken from
her.'*

My friends, Luke the Evangelist has told us a story
with which, ladies, I am sure you will identify.

You are in the kitchen preparing a meal. Your
guests have arrived and next door in the livingroom
your husband is serving drinks. He calls to you in the
kitchen: 'What will you have, darling?' But darling is
up to her elbows in cooking and carving and hasn't
the time.

1. Homily for the Sixteenth Sunday in Ordinary Time.

Your friends, of course, told you not to go to any trouble on their behalf. But all the same, you can't serve them just any old thing. And no one is offering to help. They're just sitting there chattering away and you're getting increasingly annoyed.

Two thousand years ago in Bethany, the guest was Jesus. In describing the visit, Martha's annoyance, Mary's apparent passiveness, and Christ's intervention, what is Luke trying to tell us? Let me quickly say that it has nothing to do with the choice between action and contemplation, the temporal and the spiritual, militant life or life of prayer, as common belief would have it. As if one excluded the other and vice versa! Then what is the story really about?

First, Jesus' reproach to Martha is not about her work but her agitation, and second, he proclaims once more that the priority of priorities is the Word of God.

We are 'slaves' of our worldly activities

Jesus says to Martha: 'Martha, Martha, you worry and fret over so little . . .' He hasn't said 'over nothing' because he's hungry and will want to eat shortly. He does not reproach Martha for cooking but for being too preoccupied with it and becoming its slave. This in turn will alienate her from her friends — that is, in her preoccupation with the job, she risks overlooking people.

What about us? We have to nourish ourselves, it's a duty. The Lord doesn't ignore this, he fed the crowds, he prepared meals for his apostles, he told us to pray daily to his Father for our 'daily bread.' You have to work to live and raise a family. But frequently are we not, like Martha, pressured, shoved, submerged, ending up *slaves* of our jobs and other duties?

Ladies, are you not slaves of your houses, of your children's cleanliness etc. Dust here, stains there, your kitchen floor, your livingroom draperies; vacuum cleaners, washing machines, etc. etc.

And you, gentlemen, you have repairs to your car, your wife's iron has been waiting two months to be fixed, your attic needs cleaning out; your tools, your backyard, your garage, and heaven knows what else!

We're swamped! We rush here and there, constantly short of time which we desperately need. And the more we rush around, the more out of breath we are and the less efficient we become. Until the day when a heart attack or a 'de-pression' stops us in our tracks . . . if not death itself.

And all the while, our fellow humans, our brothers, those who are nearest to us, wife, husband, *children,* neighbors, colleagues at work or in organizations we belong to, all the people around us, wait. We no longer have time for them, we don't have the time to listen; their words don't reach us any more. Monologue has replaced dialogue and we become all the poorer, shut up in our solitude.

'You fret,' said the Lord to Martha. 'You fret,' says the Lord to every one of us, 'while your brothers wait at your door wanting to meet you, to talk to you . . .'

The spiritually undernourished

On the other hand, two thousand years ago in Bethany, the Evangelist tells us that 'Mary . . . sat down at the Lord's feet *listening to him talking.'* The Lord himself had said that 'Man does not live by bread alone but on every word that comes from the mouth of God.' To those who told him one day that his family had arrived and was waiting for him, he said: 'My mother and my brothers are those who listen to the word of God and put it into practice.'

Do we listen to this word? We wouldn't want to miss the words of such and such a politician on the radio; we wouldn't want to miss a particular debate on television. That's fine. But are we as avid to listen to the word of God?

Some time back a film was called *The Big Feed,* [1] that revealed our mentality in a most fitting way. While we suffer from all kinds of digestive disorders brought on by 'terrestrial overeating,' are we not at the same time spiritually undernourished?

God speaks

God is not the eternal silence that some people complain he is. He spoke and he speaks. St Paul has told us that after God spoke through the prophets, he spoke through his son Jesus Christ and Jesus Christ broke the silence of mystery for us. He revealed the Father, and proclaimed the Good News through hu-

1. A French film entitled 'La Grande Bouffe.'

man actions and words. The Evangelists have given us the essence of these actions and words in the little book from which we read a passage on Sundays. Are we familiar with the Gospel, we who declare ourselves Christians — that is to say *of Christ?*

Have we had the intellectual honesty to read a few serious articles, or even a book, on how to read and meditate on the Scriptures? But at the same time, do we believe enough to go to Church, whether on our own or in a group, to place ourselves before the Word of God, simply, like little children who come to learn and be nourished?

God, like all lovers, desires only one thing to reveal himself to those he loves. He awaits us with a bouquet of flowers and words of love on his lips. But we don't turn up . . . we're too busy in the kitchen, we're anxious . . . and consequently unavailable.

We have no time to listen to him

I can hear some of you say: 'We would very much like to bow at the Lord's feet, but we haven't the time.' Is this quite true?

—Perhaps we only have fifteen minutes to read the newspaper. Well, perhaps sometimes it would suffice to just read the headlines.

—We always have ten minutes to spare for a bit of chit chat about the weather with our neighbor next door or our friends. Five minutes would be enough, and they could be used for a warm handshake, a friendly smile and a few words of concern.

—We spend a good couple of hours at a 'highly important' meeting. Surely an hour and a half would be more than enough provided we used the time well, to discuss things in depth and decide on a course of action.

Others will go on to say: 'It's not our fault. We live in crazy times. First you have to fight for better living conditions and then the problem will be sorted out.' Indeed! It's true that you have to fight with all you have, but is that enough?

If we are not careful there will always be a tiny transistor at the bottom of our hearts, permanently powered by long-life batteries and churning out assorted banalities, while foolish figures dance on the screen of our imagination.

If you don't know how to be recollected, even in the midst of your most worldly activities, or when engrossed by your most just and generous actions, you will never hear the Lord's Word ring within you. You may listen to the Word, read it, share it, but it will take root only in fertile ground.

A holiday for re-creation

My friends, many of you are on vacation. Some of you have returned. Others haven't gone yet. And yet others will not be going at all. I am thinking particularly of those of you who are sick and those who are too old. Instead of lying on warm sandy beaches, you will be lying in bed or sitting in an armchair by the window.

Whatever your circumstances, would you like to try to give yourself another kind of holiday, a time for 're-creation.' It's such a pleasant word! A little time to exist, to love, to contemplate. A little time to listen to another voice, the one near you which has so often shouted, or whispered, 'You're not listening to me!'

A little time longer, perhaps to listen to this God who speaks to us. It seems to me that today he is saying, 'Live, eat, work, fight, relax. It's necessary and it's good. But stop worrying and fretting. From time to time, stop, if only for a few minutes. Be silent. I, your God, want to speak to you: *I have something to say to you.*'

Jesus in the Desert or the 'Other Aptitude'[1]

The Gospel of Jesus Christ according to
St Mark — 1:12 — 15

[Jesus had just been baptized.] Immediately afterwards the Spirit drove him out into the wilderness and he remained there for forty days, and was tempted by Satan. He was with the wild beasts, and the angels looked after him.

After John had been arrested, Jesus went into Galilee. There he proclaimed the Good News from God. 'The time has come,' he said, 'and the kingdom of God is close at hand. Repent, and believe the Good News.'

Jesus has a lot of work before him. He must, as to-day's Gospel tells us, 'proclaim the Good News by saying: The Kingdom of God is here! Be converted!' He hasn't a minute to lose. The entire world has need of him. However, at first glance it would seem that he is badly organized and wasting time.

— First, his coming on earth was not very well timed. He should have waited for the coming of Concorde to help him get around faster, for tele-

1. Homily for the first Sunday of Lent.

vision through which he could address millions
of people at the same time, for computers to
keep track of all his followers, draw up profiles
and compute their needs, etc.

—Secondly, he seems to be dragging his feet. For
thirty years he remains an unknown, a simple
workman like any other, doing absolutely nothing to make any sort of impact. When he finally
decides to speak up and take action, he hesitates
over what methods to use. He is 'tempted' to
choose purely human methods, those of might
and power. So he retreats and prays to his
Father in long periods of silence. The Evangelists tell us, symbolically, of his forty days in the
desert.

What a lot of lost time! It's very puzzling. But perhaps we don't understand his way of reasoning. Perhaps there is another method of getting things done
that we don't know of, that differs fromt the business methods we know so well.

This is what I want us to try and understand today,
by reflecting on a few aspects of this 'other aptitude,'
that of prayer.

What is the use of prayer?

Who among you has not at one time or another
said or thought: 'What good is praying? What does it
offer us?' To begin with, the question is wrongly
phrased. It implies that prayer is reduced to the level
of a small business deal: to try and obtain as much as

possible from God, for ourselves and others. This is to reason like a businessman who seeks to increase the number of his contacts and cover his needs as far as possible.

'I know many people in high places, I can always get the help I need.' And if I can include God in my list, then I may be at rest. He will help me pass my exams, find a job if I'm out of work, make me well if I'm ill. When I'm nominated, he will see that I win the election, he'll bring peace where there is war, and so on. I trust him, I put myself entirely in his hands.

Such a deformation of prayer leads to grave consequences. It has a paralyzing effect and, in extreme cases, can become a drug.

If, in a general way, our relationship with God is built on such a basis, it is distorted right from the start, just like a declaration of love which begins with 'What are you going to give me?' and where the intensity of the words 'I love you' would be in proportion to what we have got out of it. In this case, there is no love for another, but only love of self — i.e. I love myself so much that I do my best to use you and get what I can out of you.

Praying is first of all 'being there,' freely, for God

Praying is the opposite to what I have just described. From the start, it demands nothing. But, it must be admitted, we are used to 'wanting,' 'possessing'; we are increasingly prisoners, alienated by a society which is entirely organized on profit so that we become daily more incapable not only of living but of understanding the meaning of giving and thus of authentic love. Let me give you an example.

Ladies, I'm sure you've all experienced this: some night at home while you are washing up, doing the ironing, or whatever, your husband says to you, 'Leave that till later and come and sit down.' You hesitate — you've so much to do. And in any case you know that a few minutes after you sit down, he'll pick up the paper and start reading or turn on the TV, seeming quite indifferent to your presence. So then you dig your heels in: 'I'm up to my ears in work and I'm wasting my time.'

But you won't waste your time, you know. Because if working for your children, your husband, your friends, is a measure of your love for them, there is also another way of loving. Not by 'doing' something for someone but by just being there, voluntarily. This is the most precious thing you can offer — your time, a little of yourself, that infinite richness of a few moments of total presence.

It is primarily at this level that prayer operates: recollecting yourself in the full sense of the word — that is, taking your whole life in your hands, the life of your body, your heart, your spirit, and offering it completely, freely and gratuitously to God; being there for him.

Then, and only then, will you be on the way to understanding the true power of prayer, one that transforms you and strengthens you for action.

Prayer transforms us

Permit me another comparison. I live by the sea. In the summer, the beach is crowded with people. I often ask the younger ones whose great preoccupation is to get a tan, 'How do you do it? You lie there on the sand nearly naked exposing your body to the rays of the sun. You daren't move because if you do you won't tan as fast, but you feel that nothing is happening. But when you take off your bikini, you can see that you have in fact tanned!' Well, prayer and especially meditation are very much like that; to be capable of stopping even for just a few moments, stripped of all that is artificial in us, our 'clothes,' our disguises, and to present ourselves naked and immobile before God to bask in the sun of his love. Here too we might feel that nothing is happening, that we're wasting time, but time given to loving and being loved is never wasted because love is life-giving.

In prayer, God gives us his life.

Some time ago I was having a conversation with a young man whose life had not been exemplary, to put it mildly. However, he had met a girl whom he truly loved. Astonished to see him so changed, so different, I asked him, 'What has that girl done to you?' 'Nothing,' he replied, 'She *loves me!*' When love reaches us, it transforms us. When God's love touches us, it liberates and recreates us.

My friends, you can't get a tan without exposing yourselves to the sun. Similarly, you can't truly be renewed without exposing yourselves to God's infinite love.

Prayer strengthens us for action

There are two kinds of energy in the world capable
of multiplying man's forces a hundredfold by ani-
mating all his actions and his struggles. On the one
hand, we have interest, ambition, pride and envy
which are manifestations of self-love; and on the
other, love of others, which is, consciously or not,
love of God.

But selfish love of self focuses our attention on
ourselves to the detriment of others and is totally de-
structive. Only true love, reinforced by individual
and collective service to others, builds up the individual and the world.

To pray is to welcome in ourselves the energy called
Love, or 'grace' as theologians call it.

To pray (whatever the form of the prayer) is to
quench our thirst at the source of Love: God. 'God
IS love' St John tells us. And this love unites us deep-
ly, converts us, makes us turn away from ourselves
and towards others; it inspires us to take up the struggle for a better world. For what distinguishes the
Christian is not the choice between fighting and refusing to fight (that's a false problem), but love as a
basis, a lever against egoism in ourselves, in others,
and in all structures of society.

*Prayer does not demobilize man; it sends him into
battle*

My friends, let us not, above all, reason like
pagans. We must not suppose that prayer will magic-

ally solve all our problems; that as soon as we call on God, he will miraculously remove all obstacles from our path like a father saying to his child, 'Leave it, my child, you'll get too tired. Daddy will finish your work for you.' In that case we would have an appallingly paternalistic God who would only kill our manhood. He wouldn't respect us and therfore wouldn't love us.

Prayer doesn't preclude effort. It puts us in a state of grace, awaiting God's action. It returns us to life, but much stronger because our weaknesses have been united with God's strength. The obstacles remain and, except in rare cases, do not change. It is we, through the grace of God, who change, take up our human battles again and win.

Jesus Christ didn't waste his time in the desert while praying to his Father. He gave himself time for love to grow in him. And it's thanks to that love that he saved the world.

As for us, in this topsy-turvy life which pulls at us from all sides, in the midst of false aptitudes and false successes, are we capable of letting ourselves be 'led into the desert?' Do we know how to be silent for a few minutes in the day, while waiting for a bus or waiting for the traffic lights to change from red to green; a few minutes in the evening after turning off the TV or in the morning on the way to work. Are we able to recollect ourselves, placing ourselves in God's axis to receive his love?

If not, we will just keep falling off balance.

But if the answer is yes, we will discover another aptitude — that prodigious aptitude called true prayer.

The Transfiguration or the 'Other Face'[1]

The Gospel of Jesus Christ according to
St Mark — 9:2 — 10

Six days later, Jesus took with him Peter and James and John and led them up a high mountain where they could be alone by themselves. There in their presence he was transfigured: his clothes became dazzlingly white, whiter than any earthly bleacher could make them. Elijah appeared to them with Moses; and they were talking with Jesus. Then Peter spoke to Jesus: 'Rabbi,' he said 'it is wonderful for us to be here; so let us make three tents, one for you, one for Moses and one for Elijah.' He did not know what to say; they were so frightened. And a cloud came, covering them in shadow; and there came a voice from the cloud, 'This is my Son, the Beloved. Listen to him.' Then suddenly, when they looked round, they saw no one with them any more but only Jesus.

As they came down from the mountain he warned them to tell no one what they had seen, until after the Son of Man had risen from the dead. They observed the warning faithfully, though among themselves they discussed what 'rising from the dead' could mean.

---

1. Homily for the Second Sunday in Lent.

My dear friends, there are many who regret not having known Jesus the way they know their friends today. If only they could have lived with him, how easy it would have been to love him and follow him . . . or so they think. In fact, it is an illusion. The Gospel today reveals that only long months after the apostles had joined Jesus did they discover his true identity.

It was on the Mountain — that high place where God, in biblical tradition, reveals himself — that Jesus showed his true face to his apostles, but most of all that's where he opened their eyes. Beyond the clothes and the flesh, they 'saw' the invisible; beyond the silence they 'heard' the inaudible: 'This is my beloved Son.'

But it was only momentary.

When the light in their hearts went out, the apostles saw only a man's face, heard only a man's words. They had to continue living by their faith alone just as we do today. They saw Jesus' face tired after long journeys, discouraged by the incomprehension of his people, sweating from anguish to agony, covered in blood and spittle, distorted by pain, and finally, a face frozen by death.

Beyond all those faces they had to find the face of the Son of God. They never completely found it, or recognized it. But later, the Holy Ghost was to cure them of their partial blindness.

And we, would we have recognized him? But it's not our problem, we say. Jesus of Nazareth is no longer physically among us. On the other hand, countless people are all around us. We look at them, they look at us . . . and we don't see their 'true faces' because we're disguised, we wear masks. We don't see their 'other face' beyond the flesh, the one that only a look of faith can reveal: their Son-of-God face. Because since God in Jesus Christ took the face of a man, man in Jesus Christ has taken the face of God.

O man, where is your face!

Man's masks and his 'real face'

My friends, who among you has not experienced the discovery or rediscovery of a person near you? When one day you exclaim (whether disappointed or thrilled), 'I've finally seen his true face!' And sometimes, you might add, 'He was so different — almost *transfigured!*'

Few men reveal their natural face; few men display the face of their soul. Why are we so anxious to hide from ourselves and from everyone else? Why so many disguises and deceiving masks? Secret men who never reveal their identity. Paralyzed men who are afraid of themselves. Hearts are buried, lives are repressed, only jerkily expressing themselves now and then through boasts, aggression or biting irony.

And why are we so quick to put masks on other people's faces? 'That man looks shifty,' 'That woman is really evil,' 'That boy will never come to any good,' we say. The mask of the liar, the mask of the wicked, the mask of the lazy . . . All these masks of the human carnival imprison people in *roles* and prevent them from becoming the *persons* they should be.

Why does society with its powers of information, education, propaganda, publicity and more, impose our behavior on us? We are constantly told: 'If you want to think well, vote well, if you want to be happy in your home, succeed in your business, have clean breath, silky hair, a slim waist, a whiter wash . . . buy this, eat that, listen to this, vote for that . . .'

Our experts in political conscience, economy, aesthetics and so on, have prepared all our disguises and masks right down to the final mask in the mortuary: a pine or oakwood coffin, with or without handles, small or large cross, all relative to income of course. There are dead people and there are dead people . . . low-income, middle-income, high-income, the famous and the ordinary.

Where in all this does man come in? The human man, made of flesh, blood and spirit; original man, *because we are all prototypes,* not items off an assembly line and if we try to create people in this fashion, we will only deteriorate radically ourselves.

Where is man? The one whom God watches over and loves?

There are people who die without ever having been themselves. We must rediscover the true face of each person and permit him to develop and grow.

When I used to go camping with young people, very often we would light a campfire at night. The next morning the fire would have turned into a charred mass of wood in a bed of ashes. We would either observe sadly that what had been a beautiful sight the night before had turned into a sorry mess, or, more often than not, we would poke the ashes for a few embers, put on some twigs, blow and blow and relight the fire. Then I would say to these youngsters what I want to say to you today:

'Never forget that in you, and in every person, despite the charred wood and ashes, there is always an ember. That's where we must look for man because the ashes are dead but the ember is alive. This ember in man is *real life* which springs anew every day under the breath of the Spirit and "God saw that this was good." From this life and only from it, the real face of every person will emerge.'

The 'other face'

The Christian must go further, much further, 'beyond' the true face of man, when his masks are snatched away from him.

St Paul said in the beginning of the Epistle to the Ephesians that God had always wanted man to be his son in Jesus Christ — that is, man has always been foremost in God's thoughts, not just a mere man but one destined to divinity. This long and prodigious 'transfiguration,' the rebirth of man which is spared the 'disfiguration' of sin, began with the coming of Christ. Our personal history with our disfigured human faces as well as universal human history, has become the way to our transfigured (that is, divinized) life and face.

This prodigious destiny of man establishes his infinite dignity and the deep reasons for his struggle for total liberation:

First, his dignity. Man is infinitely greater and more beautiful than we think. Whatever the color of his skin, his traditions, his make-up or his behavior, man in Jesus Christ has always been from the very beginning the sacred Son of God and thus should be revered. Whoever we are, we should kneel down before one another.

Second, since man is so great, to damage him in any way becomes a crime, the greatest of all crimes. It becomes a duty, the greatest of all duties, to fight against all that defiles him and everything that stunts his growth. This is what Christ fought for here on earth. The value of one man is the price of the blood of Christ.

From now on, when man destroys himself by shutting himself up in his pride and egoism, he is crucifying Jesus.

From now on, when other men or bad education, pressures, or socio-politico-economic structures prevent a man not only from nourishing and instructing himself but from developing all his capacities, they will be crucifying Jesus Christ because Christ, to save man, united with him totally.

Man's 'disfiguration' or his 'transfiguration'

And so we find ourselves facing the same problem as the apostles before and after the Transfiguration. We too are disciples of the same Jesus, we too walk with him and frequently we don't recognize him. Like the apostles, we come across:

tired faces, the face of the man on the bus returning home from work; the face of the mother who hasn't a spare minute to herself;

discouraged faces like the face of the unemployed person who lines up outside the Unemployment Office, and the face of the militant person who fights alone in a sea of indifference;

anguished faces, like the lonely aged whose offspring live at the other end of the country and whose nearby relatives will only surface at their funeral hoping the service 'won't go on forever';

faces agonizing under torture like the face of the political prisoner in Chile, Brazil, elsewhere . . . and the haggard face of the Soviet intellectual receiving 'treatment' in a psychiatric hospital;

faces frozen by death, in Angola, the Lebanon, Ireland . . .

Beyond the suffering faces of our brothers, can we recognize Jesus Christ or will our recognition depend on the Word of the Father who will announce, 'He was my beloved Son!' or the Word of the Son saying, 'That was me!'

O my God, I believe in you, you who took on a human face through Jesus Christ.

O my God, I believe in man who, in Jesus Christ, must rediscover his 'real face' and begin to don his 'Son-of-God-face.'

O my God, thanks to you, man is so great . . . if only I could see it.

The Samaritan Woman or the 'Other Thirst'[1]

The Gospel of Jesus Christ according to
St John — 4:5 — 42

*On the way he came to the Samaritan town called
Sychar, near the land that Jacob gave to his son
Joseph. Jacob's well is there and Jesus, tired by the
journey, sat straight down by the well. It was about
the sixth hour. When a Samaritan woman came to
draw water, Jesus said to her, 'Give me a drink.' His
disciples had gone into town to buy food. The Samaritan woman said to him, 'What? You are a Jew and
you ask me, a Samaritan, for a drink?' — Jews, in
fact, do not associate with Samaritans. Jesus replied:
'If you only knew what God is offering and who it is
that is saying to you, Give me a drink, you would
have been the one to ask, and he would have given
you living water.' 'You have no bucket, sir,' she
answered, 'and the well is deep: how could you get
this living water? Are you a greater man than our
father Jacob who gave us this well and drank from it
himself with his sons and his cattle?' Jesus replied:*

1. Homily for the Third Sunday in Lent. This homily was based on the
1969-70 missal in which appeared the Gospel of the Samaritan Woman. It
has now been deleted. We have kept the text with the permission of the
copyright holders of *Jour du Seigneur.*

'Whoever drinks this water will get thirsty again: the water that I shall give will turn into a spring inside him, welling up to eternal life.' *'Sir,'* said the woman, *'give me some of that water, so that I may never have to come here again to draw water.'*

'I see you are a prophet, sir,' said the woman. *'Our fathers worshipped on this mountain, while you say that Jerusalem is the place where one ought to worship.'* Jesus said: *'Believe me woman, the hour is coming when you will worship the Father neither on this mountain nor in Jerusalem. You worship what you do not know; we worship what we do know; for salvation comes from the Jews. But the hour will come — in fact it is here already — when true worshippers will worship the Father in spirit and truth: that is the kind of worshipper the Father wants. God is spirit, and those who worship must worship in spirit and truth.'*

The woman said to him, *'I know that Messiah — that is, Christ — is coming; and when he comes he will tell us everything.'* *'I who am speaking to you,'* said Jesus, *'I am he.'*

Many Samaritans of that town had believed in him on the strength of the woman's testimony when she said, *'He told me all I have ever done,'* so when the Samaritans came up to him, they begged him to stay with them. He stayed for two days, and when he spoke to them many more came to believe; and they said to the woman, *'Now we no longer believe because of what you told us, we have heard him ourselves and we know that he really is the saviour of the world.'*

My friends, because this is only a short extract from the long account of the Samaritan woman, we shall not be able to appreciate its full richness.

We question our hunger and thirst and discover that they go much deeper than would seem. So let us examine them and see what can be done to appease them.

What do we hunger and thirst for?

None of us are dying of thirst but our hunger for 'earthly nourishment' is never satisfied. So, like the Samaritan woman, we run back and forth to the well of life for our little pleasures. We know what we desire: on Sundays, for breakfast, we want sweet rolls instead of plain bread, but without having to go out to the shops for them; when the novelty of our transistor radio wears off, we want a larger model and finally a HiFi set; after the scooter comes the small car, then a bigger plush model ('It's easier on my wife's bad back . . .,' we say); sooner or later, we decide that our black and white television set isn't good enough, we want a color set; our camping tent is replaced by a trailer, then a large caravan, then we decide to buy the land to put it on . . . and so on and so forth.

Is this abnormal? No, of course not. It's only right that people should benefit from technological, scientific and economic advances, but *only* when their availability is relatively equal to one and all. What is even more serious, and I want to stress the point, is that we are gradually becoming slaves of these so-called pleasures because we want more, bigger, better. We are never satisfied. No sooner have we drunk than we are thirstier than ever. Whole lifetimes are wasted chasing an elusive and impossible satisfaction.

The human heart turns into a cash register or a supermarket and this poor overloaded thing slowly begins to suffocate because it can no longer beat to the spontaneous rhythm of freely given love. Man is now ripe for remodelling by society which transforms him alternately into producer or consumer. He is on a turning wheel: production, money, consumption. He has become that slave of olden days who used to do hard physical labor — today he still lugs buckets back and forth from the well of water that never quenches.

It is not the periodic appearance of new consumer goods on the market that will free the slave of his heavy chains.

The human body, for example, has become an 'object of consumption,' a consumer product, under the hypocritical pretext of liberation. No need to advertise beef or lamb anymore. Now the meat is human: 'Eat human flesh and you'll find happiness!' Horror films scream 'We'll frighten you to give you pleasure'; and countless artists and 'superstars' offer plastic nourishment to millions of starving youngsters.

Man is seeking another kind of food and drink

I think we can safely say that happiness does not lie at the end of the consumer rainbow. More and more people are beginning to realize this. Workers are not only fighting for a decent wage and standard of living but also for a *quality* to life, at work and at home, which would permit them to blossom as humans. Many people know that we cannot grow if we spend our lives at the mercy of a handful of people, as part of the increasingly complicated wheel of society, slaves of the almightly cash sign. A few lucid and honest people are beginning to think of an alternative society, a just one, which doesn't exist yet and which has to be fought for. But don't get me wrong — I'm not saying that a just society will solve every problem and appease every hunger.

Let me give you an example. Even if old people were legislated for and given a decent pension, a comfortable home, home help and care, there would still be something lacking: the human touch, the occasional friendly visit. Who would bring flowers and a loving kiss? And anyway, if such a wonder were invented, it would be an official of some sort going around carrying out his 'job,' and the old person would be aware that he/she was just one on the list of somebody who was probably thinking 'Phew! Five more visits and I'm done for the day . . . !'

If real happiness is not to be found in the consumer marketplace, neither is it to be found in a just and perfectly organized society. Anyone who believes otherwise is either very naive or a fake.

Other hungers, other thirsts

Psychologists tell us that people generally seek to compensate for their unfulfilled desires and frustrations. Thus some people compensate by eating. The psychotherapist's job is to discover the invisible hunger underlying the visible one.

But do you honestly believe that modern man has never had it so good and that things are improving all the time? I really don't think so. In my opinion, he is unhappy and is becoming increasingly so. He is dissatisfied because he is repressed — not sexually, as some people would have us believe, but spiritually. Tragically repressed in the spiritual dimension, he drags himself around bloodlessly transforming our so-called developed world into an arid desert. Because totally developed and thus fully contented people are not only well-fed and upright, but children of God. The world that we must build should not only be just, but a friendly community, the Kingdom of the Father. Only through Jesus Christ can we accomplish this. He is the source of new life. Some know this already, others don't, but all thirst; and this thirst differs from the hollow human one.

When Christians realize how tragically man in fact is underdeveloped, they are in danger of committing two errors. The first is to take refuge in the spiritual and say: the essential thing is not earning one's bread and building societies, so let's go for the essentials and forget the rest! This way, some people who were already engaged in the struggle to make life better grind to a halt, and those who weren't doing much anyway discover a good excuse for doing nothing at all. The second mistake is to believe that our *only* duty is to fight for a just society and that if man's true happiness still isn't in sight, it's because the struggle has a long way to go yet. Some Christians do believe this. So to accelerate the pace and allow themselves more freedom, they leave Jesus Christ behind.

The solution is to be found in the Samaritan woman's well, in the three basic attitudes of this open and generous woman.

How do we satisfy our hunger and quench our thirst?

First of all, let us imitate the Samaritan woman and go and draw water — that is, let us consider our material needs. We have to live and support our dependents. But let us not, like this woman, become slaves to our thirst. If we do, we will just have to endlessly keep drawing more and more of this 'consumer water,' chasing mirages and falling back deeper into our desert. If we don't, we will see someone sitting on the edge of the well asking 'Give me some water.' This is the first thing we must do in order to escape a lonely death at the end of an illusory happiness. We can't afford to be too isolationist, engrossed in our own individual little matters. Real and complete development is not possible for a man on his own or for just one segment of society, just one nation or just one continent. We can only truly grow *together,* as people, nations and humanity as a whole.

The next thing we must do is, like the Samaritan woman, to become aware of our sins. Her ability to confess and her openness enabled her to recognize the Messiah in the stranger who asked her for a drink of water. Our greatest sin today is to imagine that we can build a new world on our own, a world which would produce a new man who would never thirst again. We are arrogant people living in an arrogant world! Consequently we are blind to Jesus who is right here in our midst, not far away in the clouds or enshrined in some temple but right here on the edge of the well of our life. If we acknowledge our sins too, we will see him in our brothers and from the muddy waters of our hearts a clear water will spring which will become 'a spring inside us, welling up to eternal life.'

And so, finally, if we have really met the Living Christ and understood that he is the same Jesus hidden in church, in the Word and in strangers sitting by water wells (there is only one Jesus), then so that people may stop being eternally underdeveloped and dying of the thirst caused by the inadequacy of earthly nourishment let us, like the Samaritan woman, run without any hesitation (why do Christians hesitate?) to our brothers and tell them: 'We have met the Messiah; it is Jesus of Nazareth, and if you drink the water he offers you, you will never thirst again.'

The Man Born Blind or 'the Other Look'[1]

The Gospel of Jesus Christ according to
St John — 9:1 — 41

*As he came out of the temple Jesus saw a man who
had been blind from birth. He spat on the ground,
made a paste with the spittle, put this over the eyes of
the blind man and said to him, 'Go and wash in the
Pool of Siloam (a name that means 'sent'). So the
blind man went off and washed himself, and came
away with his sight restored.*

*His neighbors and people who earlier had seen him
begging said, 'Isn't this the man who used to sit and
beg?' Some said, 'Yes, it is the same one.' Others
said, 'No, he only looks like him.' The man himself
said, 'I am the man.' So they said to him, 'Then how
do your eyes come to be open?' 'The man called
Jesus,' he answered, 'made a paste, daubed my eyes
with it and said to me, "Go and wash at Siloam"; so
I went, and when I washed I could see.' They asked,
'where is he?' 'I don't know,' he answered.*

1. Homily of the Fourth Sunday in Lent (the year 1969-70). This homily
was also based on the 1969/70 missal in which appeared the Gospel of the
Man Born Blind. It has now been deleted. We have kept the text with the
permission of the copyright owners of *Jour du Seigneur*.

They brought the man who had been blind to the Pharisees. It had been a sabbath day when Jesus made the paste and opened the man's eyes, so when the Pharisees asked him how he had come to see, he said, 'He put a paste on my eyes, and I washed, and I can see.' Then some of the Pharisees said, 'This man cannot be from God: he does not keep the sabbath.' Others said, 'How could a sinner produce signs like this?' And there was disagreement among them. So they spoke to the blind man again, 'What have you to say about him yourself now that he has opened your eyes?' 'He is a prophet,' replied the man.

'Are you trying to teach us,' they replied, 'and you a sinner through and through, since you were born!' And they drove him away.

Jesus heard they had driven him away, and when he found him he said to him, 'Do you believe in the Son of Man?' 'Sir,' the man replied 'tell me who he is so that I may believe in him.' Jesus said, 'You are looking at him; he is speaking to you.' The man said, 'Lord, I believe,' and worshipped him.

Amid the many reactions to the miracles retold in the Gospel, there are two extreme ones. The first is sanctimonious admiration for some sort of a thaumaturge, 'The Christ is Almighty!'; the second is scepticism, 'There must be a catch in it somewhere . . .' implying that Jesus was some sort of a Svengali or Houdini.

For different reasons, these two reactions are wrong. A miracle is an event which can be ordinary as well as extraordinary, but one which is in itself secondary in relation to its significance. It is an event through which Jesus wants to teach us something; so the most important thing is to recognize the message. This is what we should try to do with the story of the man born blind whose eyes were opened by Jesus.

First, to assure you that we are not dealing with a fairytale which has nothing whatsoever to do with us in real life, permit me to transpose the story into our current lives.

Almost certainly all of you have either said or heard someone say, 'You know, just between you and me, I was completely blind. Luckily I met So-and-So who opened my eyes. I can make sense out of my life now and I see things differently.'

This is exactly what Jesus is telling us in the miracle of the blind man. In actual fact, he is teaching us a lesson in faith:

—What is faith?

—How do we acquire the gift of faith?

—How does it change our lives?

What and whom do you believe in?

First of all, what is faith? To understand it better, let us quickly discard a few misconceptions. Being a parish priest, I often hear the following statements:

'Father, I am a believer!'

'What do you believe in?'

'A higher power.'

'Well, Mr. Smith, I would call you a deist, that is, you believe in God. But so do Moslems, Jews, and many others. It doesn't make you a Christian.'

'I've been baptized, I've had my first communion, I was even a choir boy!'

'Religious gestures and rituals don't necessarily make you a believer.'

'I love going into a church when it's empty, I meditate, recollect myself and feel much better.'

'That only proves that you are sensitive and that you need silence. Faith isn't a "Feeling."'

'For me, God is the only explanation for man's existence, the universe, life and death.'

'Yes, but faith does not solely depend on good reasoning.'

So, essentially, what is Christian faith? Exactly what we have read in today's Gospel: meeting Jesus of Nazareth and placing our faith in him.

'Lord, I believe *you*. I recognize in you the Messiah, Son of God, come to us to reveal the infinite love of the Father and to liberate us from *all* evil.' Thus, faith is believing in a person before believing in a doctrine. It is being open to love before respecting laws and commandments.

Where and under what conditions can we meet Jesus Christ and accept the faith?

Where? It's not up to us to make appointments with the Lord. It is he who will one day give us a sign. What is certain is that he will pass us on the road of our lives, 'As Jesus went along, he saw a man who had been blind from birth.' What is equally certain is that we can only meet him under certain conditions.

First, we must be poor like the blind man. But be careful, Jesus does not beatify material poverty and misery. What he is really saying is: 'Blessed are they who expect something more, who search for the truth. There are those who know everything, they have nothing more to learn. There are those who have everything, they need nothing. There are those who are self-sufficient, they are sufficient to themselves. You have to be a beggar by the roadside.'

But in the Gospel our beggar is also blind and Jesus must 'open his eyes' so that the beggar may recognize him as the Messiah. We too have been born blind. The eyes of our body, our spirit, our heart, are fundamentally incapable of seeing in Christ the Son of the Living God. We must be reborn and acquire another way of seeing. No man can give faith to another: not parents to children, nor wife to husband, nor teachers to pupils. Of course, reason and feeling can help us along the road to Jesus Christ; we can also be witnesses of the Lord on our brothers' path, but only he can open the eyes of the blind people that we are.

Doubtless some people will think that if they have no faith, it is because it wasn't given to them. This is not so. The responsibility remains entirely ours — there is no way we can reach the south of France if we are heading in the direction of Helsinki. We can do everything possible to open someone's eyes but if he is not willing, his eyes will remain firmly shut. We can be madly loved without loving back. The greatness of man, his frightening liberty, is to be able to refuse to take the path to God, and should he meet God anyway, he is free to turn the other way. And God will not respond with pressure or propaganda. Because God never imposes, he only proposes.

How does faith change our lives?

How does faith change our lives? Well, in the same way as being able to see would affect a previously blind person. The road in front of him remains the same and so do his surroundings and the people he knows — the difference is that now he can *see them* and he can see *where he is going*.

Many people today accept life without seeing. They don't ask themselves any questions any more.

My friends, why are you living? Why do you spend a lifetime getting up every morning to go to work? Why are you trapped in this nine-to-five routine which more and more people are beginning to hate because it's so deadening after a while and *in their eyes* no longer makes sense? They are blind. Why are you living?

Many of you will answer: 'For our children.' True, but you would merely be brushing the problem aside and not really answering my question. The same problem will confront your children eventually and it will be more dramatic in their case because, increasingly, the younger generation are refusing to live without knowing what they are living for. What answer do you give them when they tell you: 'I didn't ask to be born!' One of the deepest causes of their confusion is the fact that we want to teach them ways of living without giving them reasons for living. Why live?

Others — unionists, the politically minded and other militants are fighting for a better world. This just and necessary battle gives their existence a reason but not a complete answer if they stop short of the dimension of the *infinite*. They remind me of a crowded ship. At sea, a handful of generous people do their best to keep the ship in order, helping passengers to organize themselves, to respect each other, all equals in their dignity, in the service of one another. But the ship long ago broke its moorings and lost its compass. No one knows where it has come from or where it actually is, or where it's going. It's a ghost-ship condemned to sink into oblivion.

No, the problem hasn't been resolved. The human drama lies in the fact that more and more people are overcome with the anguish of leading a meaningless life.

Another way of seeing

We need Christ to open our eyes for us. Faith —
this recognition of Jesus and acceptance of his light
— helps us to acquire his 'way of seeing,' his 'point
of view,' that is, another 'way of seeing': to see as
God sees.

To see that man does not stop at man, that he must
become not a technically and scientifically almighty
Superman but a son of God, living as he lives, loving
as he loves.

To see that the universe must be mastered by the
collective efforts of men engaged together in the
work of humanity, but also discovering that these gi-
gantic efforts are part of a Creation which is continu-
ous and must — if obstacles and vicissitudes are to
be avoided — be followed by God the Creator who
has been here since the beginning of time.

To see that the history of humanity is the slow
progress of all men towards their unity, the painful
birth pangs of the great Body of Christ which must,
in the words of St Paul, 'reunite in him all things of
heaven and earth.'

To see that suffering and death, these two inexpli-
cable monsters, were conquered by Jesus Christ, not
by suppressing them magically but by experiencing
them and emerging victorious.

To see, finally, that everything participates in this
prodigious adventure: all of us, all events, all actions,
whether they are forces of regression and death or
forces of progression and life, all are indispensable
parts of a whole.

Yes, faith changes everything. Through faith I
know who I am, where I am going with my brothers,
and why I am fighting!

O Lord, open my eyes that I may see.

The Wheat Grain that Fell on the Ground or the 'Other Life'[1]

The Gospel of Jesus Christ according to
St John — 12:20 — 33

Among those who went up to worship at the festival were some Greeks. These approached Philip, who came from Bethsaida in Galilee, and put this request to him, 'Sir, we should like to see Jesus.' Philip went to tell Andrew, and Andrew and Philip together went to tell Jesus.

Jesus replied to them: 'Now the hour has come for the Son of Man to be glorified. I tell you most solemnly, unless a wheat grain falls on the ground and dies, it remains only a single grain; but if it dies, it yields a rich harvest. Anyone who loves his life loses it; anyone who hates his life in this world will keep it for eternal life. If a man serves me, he must follow me; wherever I am, my servant will be there too. If anyone serves me, my Father will honor him. Now my soul is troubled. What shall I say: Father, save me from this hour? But it was for this very reason that I have come to this hour. Father, glorify your name!'

A voice came from heaven, 'I have glorified it, and I will glorify it again.'

1. Homily for the Fifth Sunday in Lent.

People standing by, who heard this, said it was a clap of thunder; others said, 'It was an angel speaking to him.' Jesus answered, 'It was not for my sake that this voice came, but for yours. Now sentence is being passed on this world; now the prince of this world is to be overthrown. And when I am lifted up from the earth, I shall draw all men to myself.'

By these words he indicated the kind of death he would die.

I want to teach you the secret of happiness. How to live 'another life' with Jesus Christ, beginning right now and forever — that is, to escape death — not physical death which is just another stage in life — but real death, final and definitive.

Jesus Christ tells us that unless a wheat grain falls on the ground and dies, it remains only a single grain; if it dies, it yields a rich harvest.

The wheat grain represents Jesus. What happened to Jesus? The same thing that happens to any militant person who dies for having said too much and done too much.

Christ was a revolutionary in his time, his presence was a threat to authority, he changed and upset everything, even religion. So he was spied on, followed, and there were even attempts to arrest him. One night, a friend betrayed him and the arrest was official. After a parody of a trial, he was sentenced. He was tortured not for information but out of sheer hate. Then he was executed.

Did these men succeed in taking Christ's life? Absolutely not. Because even when he was nailed to the cross, Jesus was free in the true sense of the word. The tragedies which befell him (he wasn't a Buddhist monk committing suicide for humanity) didn't overpower him in any way. He remained the master of the situation. At the very moment when they thought they were taking his life, Christ in fact saved it by offering it freely to his Father for the redemption of his brothers: 'Father, into your hands I commit my spirit.'

It is this life, the life of Christ resurrected, the life that escaped death, which is to be found at the heart of 'heaven' and earth. Man has only to open himself to Jesus and enter with him into the great feast of Easter — that is, the passage through death which leads to a joy and a life that cannot die. How do we do this? By reflecting a little more on life and death, then on love as the only means of liberation from this death.

Nobody has given life to himself

Not one of us can claim to have given life to ourselves. Life is received and it is received daily. It comes from God (we are not a river without a source) but through others, since the beginning of time. We live because they relinquished their own lives and transmitted them to us. We are enriched by their endowments but also impoverished by their egoism. We are spared nothing just as future generations will not be spared the consequences of our actions be they good or bad.

Where does real death come from?

We are not absolute proprietors of this received life. We have no right to keep it. We must receive it, cultivate it, and in turn hand it over freely. If we hold on to it, it dies because it needs circulation to stay alive, just like a river which, when blocked, will become stagnant, rotting, and die. It is man who introduces real death into this world. Man is the murderer of life. In Christian terminology, this is called 'sin,' and to an extent, 'mortal' sin, the one that causes our death. We thus isolate ourselves from the current of life, we no longer give life nor do we receive it. We are the diseased who have infected humanity.

Love the liberator

The only infallible means of escaping this progressive death is to love. Loving does not mean keeping one's life for oneself but giving it.

I always tell young people in discussions about love that it's a pity there is only one verb to describe loving: I love Jane, I love Tom; I love strawberry jam which isn't true because I don't love strawberry jam. I take it, eat it, and so destroy it. In fact, it's myself that I love.

Sometimes we love people the way we love jam. We take them for our pleasure, on a physical level or on a spiritual level. We have to constantly examine the quality of our loves. Loving is quite the opposite: because I love you, I give you a few little gifts, a little of my time, of my tenderness, of my life. Loving is always giving life to the other and receiving it if he returns it.

But no one can give life unless he gives it up. For example:

—Someone is sitting alone in the corner. I go towards him or her. I 'give up' ten minutes of my time, of my life, which I could keep for myself, and give them to him or her for nothing.

—Older children ask their parents' permission to go on vacation with a group of their friends. Father and mother 'give up' the joy of keeping them home a little longer. They give them life, their life, so that they may have one of their own.

—An involved militant worker refuses promotion so as to stay and fight on with his fellow workers. He 'gives up' a chance of a more comfortable life for the good of his brothers.

In all cases there is the gift of life, but by way of death. He who voluntarily accepts this route and lives it with Jesus Christ dead and resurrected, enters into the 'other life,' here on earth and for ever. St John puts it in a striking way: 'He who doesn't love lives in death' and 'We know that we have passed from death to life because we love our brothers.' Thus, anyone who seeks a full life must love.

Liberate life!

My friends, I don't know if you feel the way I do but I find that loving in such an authentic way is very difficult. Personally, I can't always manage it. So, and I would guess this happens to you too, I suffer the consequences.

Why is it that at times we get tired of living? Because we're not living to full capacity, we function with only twenty-five or thirty per cent of life. The rest is unused, locked up deep inside us somewhere. Why do we so often have an aftertaste of death? Because we are weighed down by fragments of our dead lives which block out any happiness we might experience. We tend to cling to past happy memories and keep them firmly in the present. All kinds of suffering, whether light or heavy, and painful pieces of a tragic life, are bottled up within us and poison and embitter our lives. All that is, and all that we have not given or accepted:

Ourselves: what we are and we are not — oversensitivity, not enough intelligence, sickness, old age, etc.

Others: the home we had or the home we didn't have; my husband, my wife ('not the person of my dreams'); the third child we didn't really want to have; or simply, my neighbor, my colleague, and so on.

Events in my life: the kind of education I received, the exams I failed, the move to another town, my daughter's wedding, my grandchildren living far away, my uncle's death . . . etc.

Be careful my friends, it's not a question of resigning ourselves — Jesus Christ didn't passively resign himself to what was happening to him. Rather, we must fight all that is bad with all our strength, individually and collectively, but *we must also know*

when to let go, burying nothing, keeping nothing.
Otherwise things would fester in us, rather like badly
digested food which eventually provokes an ulcer;
like a grain of wheat which refuses to die and con-
demns the ear of corn; like a Christ who refuses to
offer up his suffering and blocks redemption.

Let us all search ourselves for all the things we
haven't given or been able to give, for months, perhaps even for years. Let us lift our tombstones, bring
out these aborted pieces of our lives, offer them to
Jesus Christ and enter with him into the great tide of
resuscitated life — we will never die again!

What good is life if we can't give it? Jesus told us
that anyone who clings to his life loses it but that anyone who gives it keeps it . . .

My friends, that is the secret of happiness.

Have you Given Life to your Children?[1]

The Gospel of Jesus Christ according to
St Luke — 2:41 — 52

Every year his parents used to go to Jerusalem for the feast of the Passover. When he was twelve years old, they went up for the feast as usual. When they were on their way home after the feast, the boy Jesus stayed behind in Jerusalem without his parents knowing it. They assumed he was with the caravan, and it was only after a day's journey that they went to look for him among their relations and acquaintances. When they failed to find him they went back to Jerusalem looking for him everywhere.

Three days later, they found him in the Temple, sitting among the doctors, listening to them, and asking them questions; and all those who heard him were astounded at his intelligence and his replies. They were overcome when they saw him, and his mother said to him, 'My child, why have you done this to us? See how worried your father and I have been, looking for you.' 'Why were you looking for me?' he replied, 'Did you not know that I must be busy with my Father's affairs?' But they did not understand what he meant.

1. Homily for the Feast of the Holy Family.

*He then went down with them and came to Naza-
reth and lived under their authority. His mother
stored up all these things in her heart. And Jesus in-
creased in wisdom, in stature, and in favor with God
and men.*

Who would have believed it? This child Jesus, so
gifted and well-balanced, so affectionate towards his
parents, runs away and, worse still, during a pilgrim-
age! When his parents finally find him, he is amazed
at their worrying: 'Didn't you know I must be busy
with my Father's affairs?'

Mary and Joseph didn't understand what he was
talking about. All the same, they respected the freedom of this child who seemed more like an adult.
They trusted him but were still anxious — especially
his mother. And they were to suffer in silence.

You too are anxious

Parents and grandparents, many of you are worried and perhaps even disoriented by your children's
and grandchildren's attitudes, especially when they
begin to leave the nest. I understand how you suffer,
especially during holiday periods. So instead of a
homily, that is, a meditation on the Gospel, I want to
offer you some thoughts to help you, in your faith, to
understand these children who perplex and worry
you.

You don't own your children

In the Gospel we have just read, Jesus, through his manner and words, is telling his parents that he doesn't belong to them.

I'm not comparing your children to Jesus. However, they do have one thing in common: they don't belong to you.

Why? First of all because the life you gave them was given to you by your own parents, and your parents received their life from theirs, and so on. In other words, you have transmitted a life that came to you from *one Father only who is God*. You were fully responsible for this life but not its proprietor. And neither are you proprietors of your children.

Secondly, you yourselves say: 'We *gave* life to our child/children.' If you *gave* them life then it belongs to them and when they grow into young adults, it's for them to do what they choose with it. But aren't you frequently tempted to take back what you've given? Do these remarks sound familiar to you?

'You're not going out again! Can't you stay at home with your parents for a change?'

'Oh, I see! Your friends are more important than us . . .'

Your children are free to 'steer' their lives as they choose

God gave man life and the whole earth. More than any other father, he would have the right to say to his children, 'Move over. I know better than you.' However, he leaves them entirely free to conduct and to *transform* what he has given them. With us this isn't always the case.

There is in fact another way of indirectly taking back what we have given to our children and that is to give ourselves the right of intervening in their lives. I know that you often feel (and justifiably at times) that they are wasting all you have worked hard to give them every day for many years, and it's hard to come to terms with it. We intervene, you say, for their own good. And you either intervene directly or in a more roundabout way with, 'I know it's none of my business, but . . .,' or 'I don't want to interfere, but . . .' Or else you play on their emotions, 'If only you knew how much pain you're causing me,' or 'You don't realize how ill you're making your mother.'

But don't misunderstand me — I'm not saying you should shut up and look the other way. In any case, there are silences accompanied by long sighs which condemn more effectively than words. Your children should know exactly what you think and it should come from *you*. You might say, for instance, 'Son, you know we don't agree for such and such a reason. But you're a man now and you're free. It's up to you to take responsibility for yourself.' That's all. All that remains is to be welcoming and available to your children, without resentment, even if your child doesn't do what you'd like him to do or what he should do.

Here is an infallible test to see if you have truly *given* life to your children. If one of them came to you one day — *because he knows he can come to you* — and confessed that he was ashamed of certain things he has done, what would your immediate reaction be? Would you open your arms and gently say 'My poor child, how you must have suffered!' If the answer is yes, than you have given him life and are renewing it by welcoming him with open arms.

That is what the Lord has done with you. We waste and plunder the life he offered us but nevertheless he opens his arms to us, he accepts us with all our sins. This is loving someone, this is *saving* someone.

Your influence is your example

You are bound to say that you can't all the same renounce all influence on your children. No, not all influence. But you can renounce strong pressure. The only legitimate influence you can exercise on your children when they have reached adulthood is by your example, beginning with conjugal unity. This is the prime example which should run through your children's upbringing. What God has joined let no man put asunder. These were Christ's words and He knew what He was talking about. Being separated doesn't just mean going your different ways. It also means couples who walk together without ever meeting.

I don't object to alternative ways of forming families, I don't object to new methods of education —in fact I'm all for them. But we can't change the fact that a child is made up of both its mother and its father. You can't separate the two. The child is your love made flesh and if that love goes awry, the child is inevitably torn apart. You would need an awful lot of love to stick the scattered pieces together again.

The young must help their parents to 'put them into the world'

To conclude, what can I say to young people? Two things I consider essential: first, help your parents 'put you into the world,' and secondly, make their love succeed.

When Jesus had politely but firmly stated his true identity and the obligations imposed by his Father's mission, he went back to his parents and remained as gentle and loving as ever towards them.

It's true that young people must *progressively* acquire their autonomy. It's a difficult but necessary phase to go through which will enable you in turn, when you are in full control of your life, to give it to someone else before finally uniting with that someone to give it to a third party — your child. But it's equally true that to do this you must first separate from your parents. It is, in a sense, a second birth. The first time was when you were separated from your mother's breast. She suffered and she anguished, and you could do nothing about it. But now you can help lighten that suffering. Your gentleness and affection will tell your parents that leaving them doesn't mean you love them any less, just that you love them in a different, and better, way. Not like a child but like an adult.

Make your parents' life succeed

Among my young readers are those of you who, unfortunately, suffer because your parents are separated. I want to say very sincerely and in absolute friendship that you can save your parents' love, not necessarily by reuniting them but by showing them that you can succeed in your own life — the one they gave you.

If you have understood what I'm trying to say, then perhaps you will say this prayer which I have composed for all those who have suffered as a result of broken loves:

Lord, I place my burden before you.
I accept to be this uprooted, torn child
Because I now know who I am.
I am the link that can't be broken,
the flesh that cannot be destroyed.
I am their love which lives as long as I live.
I am they, united forever in marriage.

I want to live, Lord, so that they may live,
to grow so that they may grow,
to love so that they may love.
And, in silence, I will beget my parents,
I will raise them and I will save them in saving their
love.[1]

1. See *Meet Christ and Live,* Gill and Macmillan, Dublin 1973, pp. 136-7.

My friends, it isn't easy to be mother or to be father. When you feel discouraged think of Mary and Joseph who, despite their moments of pain and darkness, were able to love and *give* us Jesus.

Children, growing up isn't easy. Even if the flower that produced the fruit falls apart, the fruit, which contains the seed of life, continues to grow and mature. Offer your parents that greatest of joys — show them, and your Father in heaven, that you are an adult.

Is the Church Changing?[1]

The Gospel of Jesus Christ according to
St John — 16:12 — 15

*When the time came for Jesus to pass from this world
to the kingdom of his father, he said to his disciples:
'I still have many things to say to you but they would
be too much for you now. But when the Spirit of
truth comes, he will lead you to the complete truth,
since he will not be speaking as from himself but will
say only what he has learnt; and he will tell you of the
things to come. He will glorify me, since all he tells
you will be taken from what is mine. Everything the
father has is mine; that is why I said: All he tells you
will be taken from what is mine.*

Haven't we all, at one time or another, heard remarks of this kind: 'You know, you learn something
new every day!'; 'You see, I understand so much better now.'

It's not surprising. Man is a living creature, he
grows and develops. Other people, and experience,
enrich him. It's true of every one of us as it is of
whole bodies of people, groups, organizations and
movements.

1. Homily for the Feast of the Holy Trinity.

But what about Christians? What about the Church? Have we nothing more to discover and learn about living together? Is everything fixed, fossilized — the definitive history filed away in books and laws once and for all? A National Museum of little wax Jesus models with the character and dress of the times, the gestures and language of a bygone era faithfully recorded, to be faithfully reproduced?

Jesus Christ answered this question in the Gospel. This is what he told his apostles:

'I still have many things to say to you but they would be too much for you now . . . when the Spirit of truth comes he will lead you to the complete truth . . . All he tells you will be taken from what is mine . . .'

So, right from the beginning, all was not definitively fixed. Our Christianity is a living thing — it moves, it develops.

So, you say, the Church *is* changing! Well, yes and no. Let me try and explain.

First of all, the Church is a living organism.

Secondly, Christians, both individuals and in groups, are still discovering Jesus Christ. They are still meeting him and changing their lives accordingly.

1. The living Church

My friends, what is the Church if not a great number of communities of the disciples of Christ, from John Paul, the leader in Rome, to the baby whom you the parents have freely presented to God so that he might adopt it and allow it to enter the community of believers. Who could say that the Church has stopped growing when, on the one hand, she receives so many new disciples and on the other, she is reborn daily as people assemble to recognize God in Jesus Christ and commit themselves to building the Kingdom in the very heart of human history? Therefore, since the Church is growing, she must inevitably change!

The Church is changing. My friends, only the dead don't change, except to decompose. Happily, the Church is alive and this is principally why the 'human face' of the Church changes with time.

The Church changes also because she isn't an immobile fortress in the midst of a world in motion. The Gospel tells us that she is the yeast in the dough, and any baker will tell you that different kinds of flour make different kinds of bread. Jesus tells us that the Church is a seed in the ground, and every little seed that takes root begins to grow into a tree, a huge tree with countless branches sprouting more branches — a tree in which all the birds in the sky can build their nests.

I know that some of you are a bit lost in all this movement and change. You would prefer the Church, the Christians, the Bishops and the words to remain the same. You would prefer people today to be like the ones whose photos you keep in an album, their traits and gestures preserved forever by the camera at a given moment in time. But it's impossible. You must understand, though, that what changes is just the outer appearance, the outer garment if you like.

The same yeast is used to make different loaves of bread; the one seed produces many branches; the one life begets and multiplies.

'Still the same old Mom.' Those who are parents will surely understand! And mothers, whose day we are celebrating today,[1] when your son leans over to kiss you — this son who is now all grown up with a beard that tickles — you think of him as a man, but sometimes, he's still your little boy. And you're quite right because he is still the same child, the baby in diapers, the little boy with a rosy smile, the long-haired adolescent who used to put off going to the barber despite your half-joking, half-serious teasing. And if at times you are troubled or upset by his new ideas, his new way of speaking, acting and dressing, you know deep down — because you truly love him — that he is still your child and that you will always trust him.

And what about him? Doesn't he find you changed? Yet he still gives you mad bearhugs and you say laughingly, 'Stop acting the fool!' In spite of your different way of dressing and your different face (for you are older now and fashions have changed), he has no doubt that you're still the same mom he always knew.

1. Homily for Mother's Day.

Would believers love their Mother-Church any less than their earthly mother? Would they no longer recognize their Mother-Church because she's changed her dress? What did they love: their Mother or her dress?

I hear some of you seriously and sincerely murmuring, 'That's not the only thing that's changing . . .' Well, let's go a bit further to my second point.

2. Christians, individually and collectively, are still discovering Jesus Christ, understanding him and bringing him into their lives

Forgive me if I use a very simple example. When you are facing me, you can't see what's behind you, and if you want to see behind you, you have to turn your head which means you can no longer see me. That's because the human eye is such that it can't grasp everything around it all at once. In much the same way we aren't capable of understanding Jesus Christ completely, on our own and all at once. We can't see all his richness, nor can we live all its aspects. Our hearts, our minds and the sight range of our faith are not great enough or deep enough to grasp what St Paul call 'the height, width and depth, to finally know the charity of Christ which defies all knowledge.'

What is true of the Christian who gradually discovers the riches of Christ and begins to live one or other of its aspects — hence the differing spiritualities — is also true of groups of believers assembled in 'movements' of 'God-seekers' in their different parts of the world. And so it is for the different Churches — in Africa, Asia and Latin America. Each Church, through her history and particular gifts, is called to understand, to live and express certain riches of Christ which we cannot grasp as well as they.

Is the Church changing? No, the Church lives. The Universal Church lives. Certainly all has been said, all has been done, all has succeeded. Certainly the whole Revelation is in the hands of the Church. But can we claim that all has been inventoried, understood and, what's more, lived?

Would you like some examples?

Many centuries of meditation, prayer and love were needed for the Church to discover, gradually specify and finally proclaim the dogma of the Assumption of the Virgin Mary. It's a relatively recent event.

A long time ago, fascinated by the 'mystery' of the Eucharist, the Church practically asked priests to hide while celebrating the Mass, hence the screens still to be seen in some churches, which separated the celebrant from the faithful. Later on, the Church went the other way: Lift up the Host for all to see! Expose it! Include it in the processions! Finally, some time ago now, the Church decided that because the host was 'shown' so frequently, we had perhaps forgotten that it was made to be 'eaten.' Christ didn't say: 'This is my Body . . . Look at it!' He said: 'Take and eat, take and drink.'

So is the Church contradicting herself, changing her 'beliefs' as is claimed? Absolutely not, The Church forgets nothing but, guided by the Holy Spirit, is attentive to the varying needs of different people, different groups and peoples of her time. The Church lives in the present. She successively deepens one aspect or another of faith, emphasizes it and asks the Christian to live it.

'The Holy Spirit guides us in and by the Church, towards the complete truth! My friends, Christ is alive, the Church is alive, and no one can stop her growth, not even those who would like to make of her a permanently paralyzed old lady in a wheelchair which certain 'believers' could push back deep into the recesses of history.

The Holy Spirit cannot be muzzled to prevent the Church, her ministers, her theologians, her faithful, her groups of people and movements, from searching, discovering, celebrating and trying to live the multiform wonders that the Lord has given us.

Yes, Jesus, we believe in the Spirit who has always been at work in Your Church since her inception. All he tells us is taken from what is yours, he leads us to the complete truth.

The Doors of Life[1]

My friends, not one of us can claim to have given life to ourselves. We received, and are still receiving, life from others, from the universe, from God.

Not one of us would remain passive and indifferent if someone or something were to threaten that life.

This is because we have a mysterious hunger in our hearts which keeps us going — a hunger for a life which is unlimited in happiness and time.

Can this hunger be satisfied? And what could satisfy it?

'I came so that you might have life and have it in abundance,' Christ reminds us in the Gospel; 'I am the door, if anyone enters through me, he will be saved.'

When, in the course of our lives, we turn to these men who are loved or hated, admired or criticized, whom we know as priests, is it not because we feel, albeit confusedly, that they represent the 'door' which leads to the life offered to us by Jesus within his Church?

I would like us all to reflect on the subject of vocations.

1. Homily for the Fourth Sunday of Easter.

Seekers of life

When couples engaged to be married seek out a priest and tell him: 'We wouldn't feel truly married without the blessing of the Church,' it's because they want God's eternal Love to seal their own. They want God to be a witness to their union, to unite with them as he has done with the Church, and the priest is the sign, the symbol of God's testimony.

When parents bring their child to the priest for baptism ('In case something happens to him . . .,' they murmur), it's because they want this child to live beyond his temporal life. It's also because they know they were just go-betweens — free and responsible certainly — but nevertheless servants of a life of which they were not the primary source. They come to acknowledge the Creator of life: O Father, accept our child in the community of the Church! And in the name of Jesus Christ the priest opens the door to the child.

And those who are in mourning come to the priest because they don't want their dear departed to be buried like animals — they want the priest to be present before their grief and to be a living testimony to Christ's victory over death.

Finally, all of you who are searching confusedly for something spiritual beyond the here-and-now, including your struggle for a better life, by wanting the priest to be with you, taking an active part in your preoccupations, you sense that he can help you discover the ultimate meaning of your life. Because how can you live if you don't know why you are living?

My friends, to be born, to love, to live, to struggle, to die, we need God. But our God is not one who imposes himself through might and power. He is a discreet God who simply offers himself. He came to man through his Son Jesus Christ, not in the thundering light but in the silent darkness.

Jesus wanted the priest to be the sign, and the humble servant, of God's gift to the Church. It is the priest who announces the good news of life and love; he liberates man and gives him the life of Christ. He is not the proprietor of this life, merely its servant.

And so my words themselves reach you because there are people to accept them, print them and spread them.

Humans not Angels

Some people will say that a printer is faithful — he reproduces my words exactly. But sometimes priests can deform the face and Word of God. True, but let's stop dreaming of an ideal priest, a priest with a halo and an archangel's wings. Expecially as different people want different wings — wings on the right, wings on the left, wings in the middle, to say nothing of wings sprouting from the top of one's head so as to be able to ascend straight into heaven! We have no wings. We are humans. If you find us lacking in knowledge or love, instead of criticizing us, help us and pray we may become better people. After all, even Jesus Christ himself begged his apostles for their prayers. And don't be afraid. Whatever

the weaknesses and limitations of your priest, the
face and voice of Jesus Christ will always appear in
the pages of the book of your life. Because Christ
gave his Church a solid guarantee. There will never
be a breakdown.

Without a priest there is no Church

But despite her attractiveness and guarantee not to
break down, the Church isn't some kind of machine
or silent object. The Church is the faithful assembled
together, carry the responsibility for this life which
we must transmit to the world. It is a fact that without communities there would be no priests; but by the
same token, there cannot be a Church without
priests.

My friends, we need men who are witnesses of the
freely given love Jesus Christ has for his people.

We need voices to call us; at times they may merely
be feeble echoes but echoes nevertheless of this Word
which was given to us by God through Jesus Christ.

We need men who offer themselves up entirely to
the historical perpetuation of the roots of Christ's
Church.

We need men to assemble, give rise to and create
communities which we can in turn found in our
school, factories, and other different centers.

We need men who are free to give themselves to the
service of life, to keep Christ's sacrifice alive, for it is
the perennial source which has sprung up in the heart
of the world for the salvation of man.

Priests? Why not?

Two thousand years ago, Jesus asked this service of some fishermen, a tax inspector and others. They left everything behind and followed him.

Today, through his Church, he continues to ask the same services of good, sound men. Why should these men not respond? Would you young people not respond? Why?

Because it's too hard? Because things are 'uncertain' in 'today's' Church? Come on, let's be serious.

Do you think the man who marries a beautiful girl today knows what his wife's face will look like in twenty years?

Do you think that today's medical student can foresee what medical needs will arise in twenty years' time?

Do you think that the person sailing around the world knows what sun and what storms await him?

Think and reflect but don't cheat yourself

We have the right and duty to reflect and foresee but not to use our wise reflections as a pretext for not embarking. So let the Tabarlys of today's Church embark on their voyage and if some people want to sit on the prow of their ship and grumble that things are not what they used to be, or if others complain that there is too much arguing on board about the best direction to take, then let them turn away and hoist up their sails!

Where will the wind take them? I don't know. I'm not the wind. It's the Spirit which the Scriptures tell us blows where it wills. What I do know and what I believe with all my heart is that if they don't desert the ship, if they stay on board, if we all stayed on board, we would arrive together without fail because we have Jesus Christ on board with us.